BOOK OF LIFE

BOOKS BY MWALIMU HAKI R. MADHUBUTI (Don L. Lee)

THINK BLACK
BLACK PRIDE
DON'T CRY, SCREAM
WE WALK THE WAY OF THE NEW WORLD
DIRECTIONSCORE: SELECTED AND NEW POEMS
BOOK OF LIFE

CRITICISM:
DYNAMITE VOICES: BLACK POETS OF THE 1960's

ESSAYS:
FROM PLAN TO PLANET, LIFE STUDIES: THE NEED
FOR AFRIKAN MINDS AND INSTITUTIONS

BOOK OF LIFE

Mwalimu Haki R. Madhubuti
(Don L. Lee)

bp
BROADSIDE PRESS
12651 Old Mill Place   Detroit, Michigan 48238

Dedication

this book is for my
son
and his sons,
and their sons.
Sifa Zote Ziende Kwa Maisha Afrika

Contents

Discovering the Traitors:
An Introduction

This work comes at a difficult time in our lives. Comes at a period when we, as a race, are under much weight and can smell and feel the call of death in our very midst. This is odd. It is odd to be so concerned about death when we know deep inside that life is for living, is for developing, is for building, is for creating, is for loving. Yet, today, August 27, 1973 our smiles are still few—yet we do smile because we know too that we must not, if possible, convey the death to our children. We know that we must *seem* and *be* the promise of tomorrow. We know that we must be the music of days coming. We know that we must dance while we prepare to fight.

Time moves and passes many of us by leaving both the closed and open eyed, leaving the hanger-ons and the pimps of the race. And, the question remains: how do we, *as a people,* regain our rightful place in the world. Good question, difficult question, and there are other good and difficult questions that must be asked if we are to get answers and begin to prepare. We came as lovers worldwide not understanding *what it ain't*. We *attack the anti* rather than *be the pro*. We seek answers in the enemy's den and dare to lie to our mothers about our secret associations. The time for honesty has passed—it was about sixty years ago that negroes betrayed each other for recognition from the enemies of the world. It didn't get us anything then and it will not get us anything now. Except—certain defeat and disrespect. Yes, we came as lovers and left as killers. Enemies to ourselves. We have become our own worst enemy—a cliche, yes, but oh so true. We revolve around each other like aged boxers going for a last TKO. Our exercise now is leaning out third floor windows observing our part of the world speed by us; our exercise now is the daily ritual of putting on false eyelashes. Tell me, talk to me—why are we so immobile in a world of mobility? *We must question our powerlessness*. We must recognize the necessity for collective movement among so many *individuals*. It may be that the most individual of the world's individuals is the *negro*. This speaks to our defenselessness, speaks to our ignorance, our stupidity.

Any act of giving is an act of receiving. We are not weak men: we're just weakened at this moment. We'll find strength in each other—we'll reinforce each other, thus giving and receiving simultaneously. Togetherness at a revolutionary level. We are a world people. We black people exist in abundance worldwide and must begin to forge a *black world unity*. Black world unity is the only vehicle that will enable us to survive *white world unity*. However, we fall into many traps and unknowingly play games with our children's lives and mistakenly call these games jobs, positions, status, security, etc. The only job that is manda-

10

tory is working for the race. The *only* security we have is each other, working for the race together. And as long as a people do not know these basic facts, they will not function as a people and will remain *enslaved as a people, not as individuals.*

This is obvious to some. The poets know it. But the poets have become the traitors. The poets have become comfortable and published. The poets now talk of "private lives" and "my business." The poets make best seller records and sip coffee with the editors of America's leading publishing houses. They talk of the best for "my child" and about going to the Bahamas to write the next book. They too now talk of *making it* and *getting over.* The poets have become traitors. And
when you can't trust the poets, who is left?
After the fact comes the expected,
After the act come the poet and poems,
After the killing come the singer and songs,
After the funeral come the pimps in disguise.
What does U.N.I.T.A.* do with the poets who betray them?
What does P.A.I.G.C.** do with the poets and artists who betray the people?
What did the Vietnamese do about them? What type of re-education do the poets receive in China and Guinea?

Yes, we know, but we are not prepared for that here in the land of the "artists." And really are the poets worth such attention? Probably not. But when you're so close to the air, you must breathe it. Life comes in many forms and leaves in many forms also. They die. They live. We must forget them and build.

*National Union for the Total Independence of Angola
**African Party for Independence of Guinea (Bissau) and
  Cape Verde Islands

This book speaks to the void that developed in me after discovering traitors in our midst. But it also speaks more forcefully to the strengths gained in discovering in our people a new critical judgment that will not just forgive and forget those that do us harm—regardless of who they are. We *all* must face the coming test and it will not be an easy one. But, most will not recognize that they are being tested and they will undoubtedly fail. The few who pass will start the re-building. They will begin the final movement for *Kawaida* (Afrikan Tradition and Reason), peoplehood and land. We continue to work and await them and leave with you this, the BOOK OF LIFE.

HAKI R. MADHUBUTI (Don L. Lee)
POET-IN-RESIDENCE
HOWARD UNIVERSITY
28 Agosti 1973

Part 1

Positive Movement Will Be Difficult but Necessary

(for John O. Killens)

remember past ugly to memories of the *once*
to memories of the used to be
lost days of glory, the forgotten-forgiven history of the race:
when sun mattered and the night was for sleeping
and not for planning the
death of enemies.

beautiful
realpretty like morning vegetation
beautiful
like Afrikanwomen bathing in Tanzanian sun
beautiful a word now used exclusively to describe the
       ungettable
        a word used to describe roaches disguised as
          people that viciously misrule the world.
times is hard rufus & they gointa be harda
come on champ   chop chop
hit hard   hit harda   catch up   chop chop
sleep less   eat right   rise earlier
whip dust into the eyes of excuse makers
talk to yr children about meaning,
talk to yr children about working for the race.
chop chop   hit hard   hit harda
beat it   beat it   beat it   now

in this world
we face our comings as hip slaves unknown to ourselves
unknown to the actual challenges of the race
do you know yr real name?
do you know the real reasons you are here?
check the smiles on yr enemies' faces
if you can identify yr enemies
they crawl from the earth in many faces: negroes,
militants, revolutionary integrationists, soul-brother
number 15, black capitalists, colored politicians
and pig-eaters lying about their diets.

listen now listen
open yr ears we got a number for you
listen, somebody is trying to tell us something,
listen, somebody is trying to pull our minds.
it ain't magic we be better if it will listen
let the words seek greater levels of meaning
split in there   words be   beat it   beat it words
beat it   now
it ain't gypsy tales or trails
or false eyes frontin for the devil
it ain't about the happy ending of the west
unless you are reading the future wrong.

listen, no doubt you're very smart
we can tell by the size of yr feet that you dance too
doin the kneeknot best in the land also a
fashionplate always very very clean
pink on pink in pink by pink runnin hard
no doubt you're the best athlete to confront
the 20th century since beaver bill
expert ping pong player for the state department.
we're still runnin bases in the blind
& only see money loves money a money lover
but
can you change the direction of the fog with money?
can you beat the deathmakers with money?
can you be respected as a man with money?
can you beat yr momma's rapist with money?
they ready to be beat   cause
it ain't about making you a star
hanging in space reciting "art"
it ain't about becoming better flesheaters
sharpening yr teeth on yr children's future
it ain't about becoming successful actors
black faced draculas & 007's disguised as life.

listen now, listen
fighters fight that is what they do
come on champ chop chop hit hard hit harda
catch up box yourself into meaningness
fighters fight while others watch & take the jobs.
talk to yr children about meaning
kill those comic books.
talk to yr children about working for the race
outlaw television.
start a battle for yr own mind.
this is it this is it is in beat it be
got you beat if we be the best better than most
there is to be got to be, got to be, got to be
better than the best to beat the beast.

quiet world we are the people
summer's sun seen us through many winters
here son but we're stronger now still
unseen unwanted now we gather our thoughts now
clear our heads now collecting our direction now
looking closer into eachother's eyes now
seeing identity from doers now
looking toward the people that do now
getting as serious about our enemies
as we are about his holidays now avoiding deathtraps now
observe Bobo studying the history of the race
it is difficult but necessary.
check Willa Mae giving time to the community school
it is difficult but necessary.
much of what is needed will be difficult but necessary
much of what is needed will be difficult but necessary

the truest men are sane men
who met and conquered madness about 40 or 50
years ago. we called them crazy then, we called
them "madmen from the east,"
they wanted to reshape our destiny,
they wanted to refocus our way of life.
we called them "madmen from the east."
they had strange names, ate funny meals,
didn't wear $300 suits or drive $10,000 cars
or sell their mommas for the leisure of the west.
these "madmen from the east"
confronted the real laziness of our ways,
forced us to take sides,
forced us to deal with ideas & concepts of living,
forced us to work for the people of the summer's sun.

much of what we must do
will be different from the west
will be different from the frozen impersonal west
will be different from the snow filled west
will be different from the gray concrete colors of the west.
got to be different
got to be   got got to be   got to be   beat it now
got to be different from   got to be   got got to be
different from the west   got to be   got got to be
different from the west
if we prize life itself   living
much of what we do will be difficult and different
will be difficult,
will be very difficult,
but necessary.

We Are Some Funny "Black Artists" and Everybody Laughs at Us

random house and double day publish the
"militant black writers"
who write real-bad about the
"money-hungry jew" and the "power-crazed irishman."
random house and double day will continue to publish the
"militant black writers"
while sending much of the profits received from the books
    by the
"militant black writers"
to Israel and Ireland to build a nation for the
"money-hungry jew" and the "power-crazed irishman"
while the
"militant black writers"
who write real-bad about white people
can't even get a current accounting of their
royalties from random house or double day
and black nation-building never crossed their minds.

Rise Vision Comin: May 27, 1972

(for Osagyefo Kwame Nkrumah 1909-1972)

there is quietness   hear
time to regroup   time to rethink   time to reassess
the world we think belongs to somebody else.

there is quietness   hear
time to create an Afrikan-mind
time to create an Afrikan-mind in a european setting   Chaka
(if we had called the blood Afrikan 4 years ago he wd a
   had his
whole family out for the kill lookin for a crazy negro, an
   unamerican,
a communist, a no nothin tree swingin jungle waker-er   but

there is quietness   hear
shootin for the 21st century with 19th century weapons
while the whi-te boy is walkin on the moon
& negroes are runnin down to moonlounge on hot-pants
   night
we some BAD diamond wearers, you Bad brother:
badly taught
badly situated &
badly organized   but

there is quietness   hear
time to re-educate   time to redirect our limits   super
time to stop being the *buts* in the undefined, unfinished
sentences of the flesh-eaters: he's a first class doctor *but*
he's colored, she's one of the best teachers ever *but* she's
negro, he's a fine worker *but* he's black.   but
there is quietness   hear

we are what we are
we are what we are not
we are what we are going to be

we are what we are
the reflection the image the backward word world of what
the substance of that we must become the positive side of
      comin
send roy wilkins to Afrika if he don't act AFRIKAN
think him have mo wisdom than the OAU
a real credit to his race: bad credit a piece of 15th century
science fiction talkin bout his momma as if she was the enemy
a for real beatin down negro unsure of the space he occupies
if he occupies any   him show not invisible   we see rat
      through him
feel his opposite a walkin back steppin X-rated movie with
blocked vision   but
we comin

we are what we are not
think him Gulf Oil, IBM or GM the way he talk about
   industrializing
Afrika
if they took the water faucet from him he'd die of
   water-freeze

think him Dow Chemical or the Pentagon the way he talk
   about arming
Afrika
but we goin a need mo than wine bottles, promises & ray
   gun dreamin

think him Harvard or MIT the way he talk about educating
Afrika couldn't even teach a day care center if it was already
   taught

we are what we are going to be
comin sam comin willie comin mable comin jesus malinda
   pepper
now u different
comin rise risin comin talkin about doin it yoself hunh
about institutionalizing yr thoughts yr actions comin risin
   to
claim the tradition & collective culture of your world
   comin *rise*
rise junebug beat evil back into the cold Zimbabwe
expose the enemy FRELIMO u goin a do it Angola rise
   risin
now u different blood new stronger

stronger than storm bigger betta betta than a bad footed negro
in fifty dollar shoes comin runnin call u swift call u fast fasta
fasta than stolen Bar-B-Q in a baptist meetin on last sunday
    comin
live the land the purity of the first humans is in you comin
    rise
dash-on flash dodgin skyscrapers vacant lots & evil highs
with a conscious feel for earth for land for yoself comin rise
transformin reborn renurtured in purpose in goodness in
    direction new
u dynamite Musi where did u arrive from Kikuyu
where u been hidin Rastafarian which way SWAPO
what universe did u crash thru NewArk call u speed speeda
make yr own gas create yr own energy dig an escape hatch
    into us rise
redirectin our focus callin ourselves AFRIKANS
callin ourselves AFRIKAN men & women callin ourselves
    builders of the
FIRST callin ourselves stylers of tomorrow: the shape to
    come shaper
comin 21st century fly golden antelope a black lion is u simba
and the world is still here still evolving even the devil can't
stop that gave us the worse Enemy EVER: *ain't never seen
    nothin like the europeans* lost they taste fo life-living. but
they can't stop higher vision can't stop newrisin right talkin
good doin it gettin it done Afrikans can't stop organized builders
of righteousness pull the fight together Guinea-Bissau
we with u southern Sudan   fight on runnin wise Mozambique
jump quick lightin FROLIZI teach Nyerere watch our backs
    Osagyefo
guide our future Lumumba describe our enemies Garvey
we're comin Toure' comin PAIGC goin to surprise the world
    surprise
our fathers Malcolm we have mo than mouth mo than fast-talk
mo than Harvard rhetoric we are comin

23

we are what we are
we are what we are not
we are what we are going to be
comin comin risin risin to a higher beat of Afrikan movement
    comin fast
dancin hard makin sense remembering Sharpeville remembering
    Orangeburg
comin remembering yesterday's plant risin out of the earth
    fast
challenging new thoughts challenging concepts of false gods
    comin *rise*
elevator up juju blackworld vibrations beatin us into eachother
    rise comin risin thru visions of Afrikanlove rise comin feet
get back negative we comin shine fightin thru spacesun son is
slidin closer to the expected comin nationalists comin christians
comin muslims comin pan-afrikanists ancient black spirits
    comin comin
rise buba rise brothers rise sisters rise people of the summer
    comin
comin comin come in come in come in
we are here quick

gathered gathered gathered

to save the future for our children.

Hooked

the only time
the brother is sober is
when he tryin to
find another
high.

Afrikan Men

(for Hoyt W. Fuller & Lerone Bennett, Jr.)

there is a certain steel-ness about you
the way u set the vision & keep it
the way u view the world & warn us.
the coming tomorrow the limited memory of what was
the image the reflection the realness of what is to be.

our pace is faster but without wisdom
our "advances" are louder yet without movement
our mistakes are many & often deadly
yet we seek examples seek the quality of substance
while the lies drop around us
making the actors into the reactors
and even though we don't wear for sale signs
we've been bought rather cheaply, yet

we
with the limited memories have learned
not to trust the easy music
not to trust the processed food
not to trust the comfortable compromise
have learned
that love will not stop the enemies of the world
their nature will not allow them
to submit to the beautiful
& our minds quicken knowing that
if a rat is chewing at yr baby's skull
you don't negotiate you
kill it.

there is a certain stillness about you
unwilling to be pushed by the opportunities of the world
your insight into the holocaust will not permit
fastness, non-movement or mistakes
you understand that these are the luxuries of the young
& the young have limited memories.

we've now passed the dangers of youth because
there is a certain steel-ness about you
the way u set the vision & keep it
the way u view the world & warn us.

Spirit Flight into the Coming

For Amilcar Cabral (1925-1973), Imamu Amiri Baraka and
Congress of Afrikan People

Ever get tired of people playing with yr life, playing with
yr children's lives, playing with blackness, playing with Afrika?
Ever get tired of other people telling you what you shd be
doing for yr self? Ever get tired of people posturing,
posing and profiling?
We all know niggers look good   but
We don't own nothing
We don't have no land
We don't have no army
We don't control no major institutions
We don't
We don't even teach our children how to be themselves
We don't influence black domestic policy
We don't influence foreign policy toward Afrika
We are a powerless, defenseless people but we're
looking good, looking very good step now step
step now yo step now get in step brother lookin very good
The white boy make the clothes and put em on the store
    dummy
and we, lookin good—out dress the dummy
Hey step now get in step brother let's get a strong
line lookin good step on in
We are a powerless, defenseless people lookin very good
and don't even make the make-up we whiten our faces with

we don't do nothin except talk about what others need to be
doing for ourselves, while ourselves are too busy being
like others we talk about we don't want to be like
as ourselves wear their clothes better than they do, drive their
cars faster than they do, talk their language as well as they do
while it all spells out to be their as ourselves illusionize
about doin our thang and don't understand the world ourselves
live in but ourselves are down there just below
nixon's toilet eatin pig meat and lying to our
children about blackness.
Witness the negro asst. asst. to the president's asst.
going thru his post black period talkin about what
the administration is doing for the race maybe
him talkin about the Indianapolis 500.

We sick because we don't know *who we are.*
We sick because we don't have a *purpose* in life.
We sick because we don't have *direction* for ourselves.

Step in CAP: Congress of Afrikan People step in
refix the world clear the rust from our eyes
navigate the wind, expose the enemy, inform the mind
connect the black organs. Work a wonder:
make the negro black and Afrikan again—even if
we don't wanta be. We don't wanta be here, but we are!

29

Everything else is Jive! negro congressmen
can't even pass a bill to save they people. Colored general
too busy welcoming home war criminals, probably kill his
    momma
for another star star him in a John Wayne movie
one eyed negro Jewish dancer sleeping in the white house
hope him sleep there forever
dance sammy dance, dance sammy dance,
as our people gaze blankly at garbage men passing thru our
    communities
at midnight while
negro pimps fight their people for recognition from Agnew's
    momma.

Reflect the image CAP—step in somebody
shine brightness for a dead people.
show us that there is value in ourselves
prove to us that we are worth saving—heal the forgotten mind
the forgotten bodies of the east.
prove to us that we are worth saving
cure the negativism in us
provide the example teach the doctrine
display identity: we were builders of the first.
display purpose: our children, our parents, our
                    ancestors *great as we be*
display direction: sharing land, raising our children,
                    building a world the way a world is supposed
                    to be built.

Everything else is Jive: Ph.D.'s in french, can't eat no french
can't farm no land with french. wake up showboat, wakeup
    showboat
Dr. Clearhead Knowitall Ph.D., summa cum laude U of
    Chicago 1973
now teaching the *psychology of blackness* in the suburbs
proving to the enemy—that taught him—how smart him is
what have you done for your people lately Dr. Knowitall?
what have you done for the race except, race away
waving flags about it's a human and class problem
ask you great, great, great grandmomma, fool,
was she raped from a continent due to the human/class problem?

Step in Imamu:
plant the seed and regulate the growth you are the
vegetation of life. bloods are getting up earlier now
catching the sun on the second mile run getting ready
for the day's work getting ready for the heavy load
cleaning up. washing down. disciplining ourselves consistent
with nature now. getting ready to re-make the life in us,
telling ourselves how we back stepped into what we
now be. tomorrow is our coming.

Everything else is Jive: we got negroes arguing the necessity of
Marx and Engels to empty bellied children, we got negroes
    married to
white people speaking for the race. don't no Arabs speak for
    Jews.
we slaves because we wanta be. we slaves because we wanta be.
unbelievable
but being a slave is hip
being a slave in america is *really* hip
slaves think they can buy their freedom
slaves drive big cars
slaves take dope
slaves love big houses
slaves teach blackness at big universities
slaves love their enemy
slaves love death in any form
slaves love paper money
slaves live for pleasure only
if we slaves be let free we'd buy ourselves back into slavery.
it is hip being a slave in America cause we got everything
    slaves need,
we're the richest slaves in the world.

Step in Imamu
all that is good and accomplished in the world takes work
work is what we need an abundance of
work for a better value system work
work for ourselves like we work for general motors,
like we work for integration, like we work for the
son of mary work
teach one reach one work and study

study the math, the physics, the chemistry that is revolutionary
study the science of building that is revolutionary
study the inner workings of yr self that is revolutionary
think about building a liveable world that's revolutionary
meditate on a new way of life that's revolutionary
Juba Juba Juba du
move Juba into agriculture like we move in fashions
work Juba work Juba work
Juba Juba Juba du now work Juba
write some work songs Juba work
paint some work pictures Juba work
play some work music Juba work
Juba Juba Juba du
work raw honey for the brain
work exercise for the dead blood cells
work life serum for the tired muscles
work chakula for the body
work the land into food
work to keep yr woman by yr side
work the evil into good
work the enemy into submission
work and organize   organize the work
work and develop   develop the work
work and study   study the work
work energizes Afrika and Afrikan people
work energizes Afrika and Afrikan people
All that is good and accomplished in the world takes work
Everything else is Jive

17 juni 1973

33

Part 2

BOOK OF LIFE

It is Afrikan
that the sayings
of the Fathers be
passed on to the sons.
It must be done
It is tradition and it is
Law.

1

the best way to
effectively fight an
alien culture
is to live your own.

2

pride in one's people is desirable
pride in black people is necessary for black people
but
pride must be properly cultivated
and displayed in moderation
too much pride alienates brother from brother
alienates man from community and nation
too little pride
confuses the natural direction brothers must take
and hinders the building of nations
pride in abundance is bad
too little pride is bad
strike a balance.

3

is a sign of life in your face?
is the sign of life in your thoughts?
is the sign of life in your actions?
if not   there can be no life in you.
if so   you are life.

4

there is life in man
man is life   but
when man puts himself above other men
life becomes disproportionate and loses clarity
when man puts material and worldly goods above man
man's understanding of and value for real life ceases
his wife becomes something he sleeps with
his children become objects to order about
his friends become competition
the land becomes property to fence in
his aim in life is toward making it and getting over
his tradition ceases to have meaning
and is not passed on to his sons
his tomorrows are now measured in material production &
    acquisition
and his future is that which he puts in the bank today.

5

he who knows
both ways
and proceeds to take the incorrect one
may not be able to reverse himself later.

6

to know is to be
to be and not know is not to be
to know and not know that you know is not to know
to know and not be is not to know
to know is to be

7

To seek all the answers of life
into yourself is to misunderstand life.
man is only a minute portion of all
that makes up life and our relationship
to other forms of life gives meaning to
our life.
we are all in the cycle of return and live.
understand yourself first but also go
outside of yourself so as to understand the
cycle of life.
seek answers of the world in the world
while understanding that the world
is part of you.

8

it is true that nature   in time
will solve the world's problems
and resolve the world's disputes
however, nature and time are unpredictable
and may not act in our lifetime.
our understanding of life
demands that we respect nature & time
but our children's future
demands that we help nature solve our problems today
with the little time we have on earth.

9

if we are not for ourselves
who is for us?
if we are men
why are other people giving us orders?

10

There is much to be learned
there is much to be unlearned
to do both
takes an open mind and a mind that questions.
we can get correct answers   only
if we ask the correct questions.

11

We have people in our midst
who can quote
every body from *can* to *can't*
but do nothing else.
theory without practice is like
a car without gas   is like
land without cultivation   is like
poetry without content.
men *act*
others re-act and talk about acting.
which are we?

12

there are men
who have never left
home
but understand the universe.

13

A man who thinks nothing of himself
is not a full man and cannot appreciate other men
because he cannot appreciate himself.
a man who thinks only of himself
has no room for others
and cannot appreciate others.
a man who is secure in himself
will not fear security in others
and
will be motivated toward the most secure of relationships
that of friendship between men
and friendship between men reinforces security in man.

14

Weak men
hide behind titles
and status to aid their egos.
weak men
attack from the rear.
watch your back
as you move forward.

15

Know yourself first
that which is good
that which is bad
correctly assess yourself
and you will not mistakenly assess your neighbors.

16

We are not a tribe
we are a nation.
we are not wandering groups
we are a people.
we are not without land
there is Afrika.
if we let others define us
our existence, our definition will be dependent upon
the eyes, ears and minds of others.
other people's definitions of us cannot be accurate for us
because their hurt is not our hurt,
their laughter is not our laughter,
their view of the world is not our view of the world.
other's definition of the world
is necessary for their survival and control of the world
and for us to adopt their view of the world is a necessary
step toward their continued control over us
therefore to let others define us is to assure
we *will* be a tribe,
we *will* be wandering groups,
we *will* be
landless
self definition is the first step toward
self control.

17

if you know who you are
the identity of others
will be respected, appreciated
understood.

18

talk little and listen with care
a man who talks much
cannot hear the silences around him
cannot hear the noises around him
he hears only his own voice
and will mainly talk of himself.
talk little and listen with care
there is more to the world than your own voice.

19

If you are silent
no one can hear you coming
if you make much noise
your enemies can prepare for you.

20

Knowledge of self starts at home
understand that which is
closest to you first.
understanding that which is nearest
brings meaning to that
which is far.

21

many people fear knowledge
knowledge stimulates change and most people fear change
to acquire knowledge is to grow
to grow is to change
growth without knowledge is not growth
growth with knowledge leads toward wisdom
there are few wise men in our time
and change is what we need.

22

If the people
think that they can buy everything or
that everything is for sale
then there is little left in life of real value.
they will spend their days making money
spend their evenings thinking about what to buy
and spend their weekends buying.
this is not normal and is in conflict with
the natural way of life,
if a people feel that they can buy everything
their values are corrupt and they too
can be bought and are not to be trusted.

23

the need of expensive clothes, cars and homes
to impress others and yourself
only means
that you have no meaning without them
which also means
that you have no meaning with them.

24

To
betray a trust
is to
cut yourself off from being
trusted.

25

to be ignorant of the world around you
is slavery
to not want to know of the world around you
is death.

26

We must be able to function within ourselves
we must build and develop our inner spirit and force.
this gives autonomy to our outer movements
as we seek to forcefully interact with the larger world.
if this interaction is to be successful
it must be a force with spirit behind it that
no one will doubt. such a spirit
and force can only come from a people who
have faith in themselves and the path they
have chosen for themselves.
we are an Afrikan people.

27

to know nothing is a statement of negative being
to know nothing speaks to a condition of uselessness
to know nothing puts one at the mercy
of those who know.

28

if you are confused
you'll bring confusion to
everything you touch.

29

a man who eats
everything that is placed before him
by anybody, anywhere
cannot be a healthy man
choose your food as you choose friends
with care and knowledge of its ultimate value.

30

to go without food
brings an understanding
of the people who are foodless
but
to go without food
and know that none is forthcoming
brings an appreciation and understanding
of food and the foodless
that is unlearnable any other way.

31

a man who eats and needs
many meals in a day
could not be eating the food that gives and maintains life.
life-giving foods such as vegetables and fruits
are the basis for good health and long life
and should be consumed modestly.
processed food from processed sources
produce a processed body with a processed mind,
produce men whose first love is to eat
and only aim in life is to
make it to the next meal.

32

Many of the modern day diseases
that hurt us did not exist many years ago.
however many years ago our diets didn't consist of:
powdered this and instant that,
frozen now and eaten later,
canned everything and contaminated water,
pour and mix and open and stir   all
preceded by any flesh of the world,
from fried monkey to boiled pig bellies,
you cannot sustain life with "foods"
out of boxes, cans, plastic and resealable jars.
you need live food for live bodies.
stay close to the earth
consume that which the earth naturally gives us.

33

There is meaning here
in us under the weight of hours today
under the weight of misunderstanding of their world.
we clench our teeth, lie to our children and make it.
but the feared breaks through
the air is dirty and kills much,
the streets are trafficful and nothing moves,
the water is impure and slowly damages the drinker.
life cannot endure this way.
there is meaning here
if we seek it.

34

The family is the basic unit of all nations.
the family structure has endured since recorded history.
the family structure will continue to survive the sickness
of the day:
let the singles come,
let the bi-sexuals come,
let the homosexuals come,
let the non-family advocates come,
let the extreme individualists come,
let the unisexuals come,
let the transvestites come.
those are brief aberrations of a sick nation
and if the nation is to live and prosper
the family will live and endure because
the nation is families united.

35

There is much special
about black women,
the way they endure,
the way they grow,
the way they build,
the way they love,
it is traditionally thought that black women
are the reflection of black men.

36

Only fools limit their women.
the full potential of a nation
cannot be realized unless the
full potential of its women
is realized.
only fools limit their women.

37

a nation cannot grow without its women
the intelligence of a nation
is reflected in its women
who bear the children for the nation
and are charged with the early education of the nation.
a nation cannot have intelligent women
unless the women are treated intelligently
and given much love.

38

The substance and mental attitude of a nation
can be seen in its women, in the way they act
and move throughout the nation being productive.
if the women have nothing to do it reflects
what the nation is not doing.
if the women have substance and are given responsible positions
the nation has substance and is responsible.

39

If a woman covers herself with paints
of blues, red, grays and yellows
she unknowingly kills her skin,
she unknowingly smothers life from the first layer covering.
to paint a flower white that is naturally red is to
close its breathing pores and interrupt its natural skin growth
the flower will soon die.
to paint black skin green, orange and other colors
is to display black skin as something that
should be hidden from the actual world
and slowly suffocated from life.

40

It is normal
for man to look at woman
but
it is abnormal to look
at woman the way we
have been taught to
look at her in the western world.

41

We have been given
only one standard of beauty which
is the exact opposite of our own self image.
due to this we see beauty in others
and fail to see it in ourselves.
this leads to destructive self-concepts that
will not only affect our relationship
with ourselves but will affect our
relationship with the world for the worst.

42

nothing is created
without a mind
that is creative.

43

Institutions that reflect and guide a people
are important and necessary.
nations are made up of people who
create institutions that give substance
to the nation and its people.
where are the black institutions that
give substance to black people?
most of us would have difficulty identifying
more than one of them.
we must have new institutions in order
to institutionalize new thoughts and actions.
we must make current black institutions more
accountable to the needs of black people whom they
say they serve.

44

We sit in our used cars
talking bad about others who don't own used cars and
we think that we are better off.
wonder who is running the world
while we talk about used cars?

45

If you are silent
few will know
your ignorance.

46

We must work to make life,
we must study to understand life,
we must create in order to support & stimulate life,
we must build to maintain life.

47

The more complex life becomes
the more confused are the people.
we live in a world where we
pay to be born,
pay to life   and
pay to die.
when the people seek work
they are computerized and given numbers,
when the people speak of hunger
they are photographed and made to feel less than people,
when the people seek medical care
they are filed into lines and experimented with,
when the people ask for education
they are scorned and laughed at,
when the people seek truth to be truth
they are lied to and ridiculed.
for those who need to know
you mistake the people's smiles for thank yous
and their sincerity for stupidity.
the people are not so soft and naive
as not to be able to remove complexity
and wipe out confusion
when they bring the hour.

48

You do not save people
by putting water on their foreheads
or by immersing them in the deep.
save people
by being and by telling them the truth.

49

Beware of quick smiles
and fast words.
one who smiles overmuch
mis-uses his face.
one who talks too fast
seldom says anything worth listening to.
quick smiles and fast words
fool the weak,
confuse the strong,
do damage to the face   and
mis-use the language.

50

best teachers
seldom teach
they be and do.

51

you
are nothing
as long as
nothing is on your
mind.

52

Let us not seek to impress our people
with the eloquence of our words.
words cannot feed the hungry,
words cannot clothe or house the needy,
words cannot heal the sick,
words cannot plant the food.
words take us away from the doing.
speak carefully and with substance
and
you will not have to speak much about nothing
if this is done
your presence will be welcomed,
the people will speak highly of you at family gatherings
and you will be sought after by many.

53

How many of our children
have seen the ocean's ripple
or have felt the morning wetness
of country
vegetation
or picked the just riped fruit from trees or vines
or enjoyed the afternoon sun bathing
their bodies as they played in the green.

there is little that is green in the cities
other than the broken stop lights and
artificial grass.
our children's dreams are lost among the
concrete of too many promises
waiting for elevators to take them
to the top floors of public housing.

54

Corruption comes because man disrupts
and confuses the meaning of life.
he reorders the natural and human
values to those of:
making money,
gaining power,
searching for sex,
pursuing fame,
seeking status
and lying to his children about life.
we need a new system of values speaking
to the real meaning of man.
corruption breeds corruption
the non-corrupt cannot live among
the corrupt and not become corrupt also,
one either leaves and exposes
or one becomes corrupt
there is no compromise,
there is no in between.

55

When you work for yourself
you must *work* for yourself.
either we use the time we have wisely
or we do not use our time wisely.
if we say that our day starts at 6:30 a.m.
then it must. if we start at 7:30 a.m.
we are already an hour behind   an hour that
cannot be made up.
our enemies work 24 hours a day and
do not have hours to make up.
there
is no substitute for work.
but
there is a substitute for talking about work.

work!

56

We do not equate
poverty with blackness
nor do we equate the lavish
use of wealth with blackness.
we now live in a time
where the many go without
while for the few we have entrusted to lead us
luxuries have become needs.

57

The cities kill the will,
dull the senses,
make white the eyes and
stop the future in us
before it starts.
if we survive the west
we survive the worst,
but let us not become
worse in our survival.

58

A people without their culture
are a people without meaning.
a people without their culture
are a people without substance.
a people without their culture
are a people without identity, purpose and direction.
a people without their culture
are a dead people.

59

The old of our people
are the elders of the race
and must be listened to,
must be looked after,
must be given meaningful work,
must be loved and cared for,
must be treated with the highest respect.
the elders of the race
are the reason we are here.

60

To hate one's self and one's people
is not normal
to perpetually wish to be like other people
is not normal
to act against one's self and one's community
is not normal
that which is normal for us
will never be normal for us
as long as the abnormal   defines what
normality is.

61

We now have in our midst
men who *only* read and write and talk or argue.
these men play with concepts and ideas,
can quote you the theory of the world,
can discourse for days on the meaning of man,
have usually an answer for everything and if they don't
have the answer they consult each other until
they come up with an answer.
these men are powerless,
these men are defenseless,
they have no land and mainly live in the cities.
they do not control major institutions
they do not control production,
they do not control distribution,
they do not make decisions on major policy for the nation,
they do not control the armed forces.
these men would starve to death if somebody else
didn't bring them their food.
these are defenseless and powerless men.
they play with concepts and ideas and
divorce themselves from implementation.
these men are not to be feared, they are to be re-educated.

64

62

A man becomes the best runner in the country
because that is what he has been taught to be
and he wishes it and works hard for it.
a man becomes the best doctor in the country
because that is what he has been taught to be
and he wishes it and works hard for it.
a man becomes the best hustler in the country
because that is what he has been taught to be
and he wishes it and works hard for it.
the major reason we don't work for our people
like we work at being runners, doctors and hustlers
is because no one has taught us to be and act as a people
or what the value and importance of being a people means.
therefore, we are busy being the best runners, doctors,
and hustlers in the country.

63

Our belief in our people
can only be measured by the
belief we have in ourselves
if we do not believe in ourselves
our belief in our people will not be real
because   we are the people.

64

Afrikan holidays
are holy days:
teach the history,
legitimize the nation,
reinforce the traditions
and
reunite the families.

65

look beyond tomorrow
it will help you
accomplish that which is needed
today.

66

You will recognize your brothers
by the way they act and move throughout the world.
there will be a strange force about them,
there will be unspoken answers in them.
this will be obvious not only to you but to many.
the confidence they have in themselves and in
their people will be evident in their quiet saneness.
the way they relate to women will be
clean, complementary, responsible & with honesty.
the way they relate to children will be
strong and soft full of positive direction.
the way they relate to men
will be that of questioning our position in this world,
will be one of planning for movement and change,
will be one of working for their people,
will be one of gaining and maintaining trust within the race.
these men at first will seem strange and unusual but
this will not be the case for long.
they will train others and the discipline they display
will become a way of life for many.
they know that this is difficult
but this is the life that they have chosen
for themselves, for us, for life:

they will be the examples,
they will be the answers,
they will be the first line builders,
they will be the creators,
they will be the first to give up the pleasures,
they will be the first to share a black value system,
they will be the workers,
they will be the scholars,
they will be the providers,
they will be the historians,
they will be the doctors, lawyers, farmers, priests
and all that is needed for development and growth.
you will recognize these brothers
and
they will not betray you.

67

a son needs direction if he is to be strong & work for the race
he does not need harsh words
about the way he should be
or words about how he should do this or that.
Fathers
study your own ways
so that your actions may guide him past the pitfalls of life
the best teacher is you being the example
of what others talk about.

68

Don't talk about
organizing the city or the world for self-reliance
when you can't organize
your own house or community.
start with self
and move to those closest to you
and each in turn do the same.
it is a slow but effective process
and it is better to be
slow and effective than to be
fast, ineffective and seen in all parts
of the city talking
nonsense.

69

We know more about
how to kill than we know about
how to save.
our medicine is curative rather than preventive.
the weapons of war are more numerous
than schools, hospitals or places of worship.
we destroy small nations to save them from ideology.
we teach our children the ways of life
as we act out the ways of destruction.
our contradictions are catching up with us
and we will fall very fast in our lies and acts
because we are ill-prepared for saving.
we know more about how to kill.

70

Nations are like people
they need each other
no nation is truly independent
all nations are interdependent
however some nations are more dependent
on other nations than on themselves
so as
to put them at the mercy of other nations.
strengthen yourself internally before you seek
strength from the outside.

71

The need to impress the world
shows little understanding of the world.
the need to make good impressions
means you have false impressions
the need to be The Best
is to misunderstand what best is.
the major reason for competition
is to take us away from cooperation and collective actions
and allows the many to be subtly controlled by the few.
put faith in the ability of each other
while weakening the weaknesses of each other.
this is the natural order of things
and you will stand out
like vegetation in the desert
and will attract much water.

72

It is said that,
"death is no threat to a people
who are not afraid to die."

yet
life today in part is controlled
by those who are afraid
to live.
a reordering of the world is due.

73

There are no vacations
when a people are enslaved
there are just more sophisticated
forms of slavery disguised as
three weeks off with pay.

74

understand the enemy within
and
the enemy without
will
be easier to deal with.

75

We love our dogs
more than we love ourselves.
we feed our dogs three times a day.
we clothe our dogs in dog clothes.
we walk and talk with our dogs every day.
we call our dogs "man's best friend."
we play with our dogs and buy them dog toys.
when our dogs get sick we see that they get the
best of care.
if we dealt with each other one fourth as well
as we deal with our dogs this would be
more of a people world than a world
livable for dogs.

76

If i make mistakes
tell me about them while i live
don't wait until i have left the earth
and then accuse me of contradictions
i may not have been aware of.

77

In seeking answers
don't go too far on too little
you may not make it back.

78

black people
are all musicians
even though
they don't all
play instruments.

79

move around wishes
and begin to control reality.
you can't wish good life upon a people,
you can't wish the best education upon a people,
you can't wish shelter and clothing upon a people,
you can't wish self determination upon a people,
you can't wish self respect upon a people.
you can't wish self defense upon a people.
replace most of your wishes with work
and you will not have time to wish often
you'll be too busy harvesting your crop.

80

Knowledge is like water
it is nourishment for those who seek it
and wasted on those who misuse it
but for all whom it touches
it does some good   so like water
let's spread knowledge worldwide.

81

If you need to learn nuclear physics
you go to a nuclear physicist.
if you need to know how to work the land
you go to a farmer.
if you need to know how to build a house
you go to a carpenter.
if you need to know mathematics
you go to a mathematician.
if you need to know medicine
you go to medical school.
when all is learned that is needed to be learned
you return to your people and set up your own
schools for your own people.
this is one way
to fight and win wars.

82

A man's world is in his eyes.
if man believes he has a future it will be in his eyes.
if man is well physically and mentally you
will see it in his eyes.
if a man is good and is to be trusted look into his eyes.
if a man is evil his eyes will not hide it.
if a man is afraid, his fear will look at you.
if a man has strength, the part of the body
to show it first will be his eyes.
with the eyes you cannot deceive
nor can you make them up as to hide
their real meaning.
most people will not look you directly
in the eye.
some hide behind sunglasses,
some hide behind just not looking at you.
the eyes tell too much.
if you seek answers about a man
do not look at his possessions or non-possessions
to tell the way of a man
look into his eyes.

83

Why do most of our leaders who
start out as a part of their people
and genuinely work for their people
end up
living away from their people and
telling their people what *they* should
be doing while getting upset because
their people question their credibility?

84

You can't define
tomorrow if you don't
know where you are
today.
if you do not read,
read!
if you do not think,
think!
add to reading and thinking
meditation.
meditate at a minimum of one hour a day
evenly divided.
1/2 at sunrise and 1/2 at sunset.
this will balance the internal
with the external and
bring knowledge of a *force*
greater than self.

85

Pimps and prostitutes
are the sickness of a nation.
are the sickness of a people.
but if a people are not able
to offer the pimp and prostitute
a tomorrow or a future that is believable
the sickness will remain
and worsen
until the death sets in.

86

Few things of value in life
are accomplished individually.
nations are built collectively,
schools are built collectively,
farms are farmed collectively,
holidays are observed collectively,
this is natural for those who have
direction and respect each other.
those who work share in the
goods produced and profits made.
those who are unable to work
are taken care of.
when the people of a nation begin
to use "I" more than "we"
the nation is dispersed and is in trouble.

87

A negative act is a lesson,
a contradiction can be learned from and
there is meaning in evil
for those who are seeking good.

88

If a man
can be bought for $50.00
he can be bought twice for $100.00
if he'll sell himself to you
he'll sell himself to others, also.

89

We wound each other
with false words,
evil eyes,
often lies
and pettiness disguised as criticism.
watch the men closest to you
some of them carry the knives
that cut the deepest   as they
agree with you while you die bleeding.
yet still,
even among the closest of enemies
the best defense
for your position
is your practicing
it.

90

How many of us can
run a mile without tiring,
touch our toes without
bending our knees,
do pushups and pullups
without damaging our bodies for life?
the body needs exercise
just as the mind needs exercise,
the mind cannot function at its
peak unless the body is physically
at its peak.
reading, studying, and doing practical research and work
develops the mind.
morning exercise, physical work
and practical eating
develop the body
the mind and the body   must work as one,
for you to be one.

91

your name
tells us who you are,
where you come from,
where you are going,
how you may get there
and who is going with you.
your name
is legitimization of the past
confirmation of the present
and direction for the future.

92

People play with the spirit
and at being "spiritual."
they cut themselves off from the real world
while meditating on rocks and water
and turning the sun into the moon.
the reality of life is confused abstractions
and the people do not understand them
and dismiss them as being crazy.
the people are correct.
meditation is needed and necessary
but must move the higher levels of the mind
into the people and not away from the people.
we meditate to maintain a balance in ourselves
while seeking greater wisdom of the outside.
it is not wise to seem abstract
when that which is practical is needed.
the most spiritual of acts
is
how positively you relate to and
work with your brother-man.